COMINGS AND GOINGS

Gatehouses and Lodges

Peter Ashley

Everyman Pocket Books
In association with English Heritage

Comings and Goings – Gatehouses and Lodges

**Published by Everyman Publishers Plc
in association with English Heritage**

© 2002 Everyman Publishers Plc
Text and photographs © Peter Ashley

ISBN 1 84159 081 9

Design by Anikst Design
Printed in Singapore

Everyman Publishers Plc
Gloucester Mansions
140a Shaftesbury Avenue
London WC2H 8HD

Lilford, Northamptonshire
(p. 1) South of Oundle is a pair of late 18th–
century 'mirror image' lodges in Jacobean
style serving Lilford Hall, angled to the lane
and the hall driveway all the better to gain an
uninterrupted view of the comings and goings.

Tusmore Park, Oxfordshire
(p. 2) These lodges are amongst my favourites
anywhere in England, and what makes them
especially remarkable is the fact that they were
completed in 1998, designed by Peter Cave for
the new house rising at Tusmore.

Please remember that many of these lodges
are lived in, and when looking at them please
respect the privacy of the occupants. Even
quite tiny lodges that appear empty can often
be someone's home.

contents

introduction *Anne passed under the arched gateway which screened the main front; over it was a porter's lodge, reached by a spiral staircase. Across the archway was fixed a row of wooden hurdles, one of which Anne opened and closed behind her.* 'The Trumpet Major', Thomas Hardy.

It is the building type with a lion's head on a goat's body, decorative, authoritative, absurd, and an unusually revealing architectural demonstration of the aesthetic games which a society chooses to play. 'Trumpet at a Distant Gate', Tim Mowl and Brian Earnshaw.

For as long as there have been buildings, there have been ways in and out of them. Not just openings and doorways, but gates that could be the first line of defence or the first line in a style offensive. Either way, they could make statements about their owners, giving loud hints about what was to follow. This pocket book looks at the gatehouses and lodges that reached a kind of golden age in the 18th and early 19th centuries. It focuses on those announcements to country parks and houses that usually lie in peaceful bucolic isolation, and which for our purposes will start with their 12th–century origins in castles and abbeys. In all cases they are independent of their parent buildings, and most were capable, at least at one time, of being inhabited.

Castle entrances were always the most vulnerable part of the defences. If Norman barons could go out, their enemies could equally attempt to get in the same way. Even with wooden keeps and palisades, the main gateways would often be built in stone, with the means to drop noxious substances on the unsuspecting heads of attackers, and room for portcullises, drawbridges, and living quarters for guards. As the gatehouse started to become the most prominent and important part of the castle, so grew the opportunity to use it as a display of not only military might but also of wealth and prestige. When the need for vigorous defence subsided, and castles became fortified homes, the gatehouse softened more into a decorative entrance, but still with the ability to keep out undesirables. Abbeys retained gatehouses for much the same purpose – as a screening device – with a porter's lodge and possibly a little chapel upstairs. By the 16th century the domestic gatehouse was becoming absorbed into the fabric of the house, gradually turning itself into a grandiose porch, albeit with tall towers and much architectural fanfaring.

But we will stay on the outer fringes, where Elizabethan garden pavilions began to take on more practical purposes. Possibly the first lodges to be built specifically as entrances to country houses were Sir Baptist Hicks' ogee-topped buildings for his house in Chipping Campden, but after the same Civil War that saw his house razed to the ground, and then the Restoration, the development of the lodge was virtually suspended for the next fifty years in favour of swaggering Dutch-influenced gate piers. And then, in the 18th century, an age of landscaping and architectural experiment saw the classic lodge mature into what has become our popular image of them as the homes of aged retainers fumbling with keys on dark windswept nights to open wrought iron gates for impatient masters. The lodge thrived with the Italianate and Gothic tastes of the 19th century, finally reaching an Arts and Crafts swan song with the vernacular styles of Lutyens and Voysey.

English Heritage preserves many gatehouses at the abbeys and castles in its care, and is actively concerned with the listing, restoration and conservation of surviving park lodges. Its work helps us to appreciate even more their unique place in our architectural history.

fighting spirits Very few castle gatehouses are now used for pouring boiling oil over visitors, and many are pale shadows of their former imposing characters. The first gatehouses were purely functional – the primary military objective before outer and inner baileys could be reached. Their sheer presence soon became a symbol of the proprietor's prestige and taste, and decorative elements that reflected this became obligatory; these ideas can be traced through every gatehouse and lodge that succeeded them.

Wigmore Castle, Herefordshire

Wigmore Castle, Herefordshire This is how a ruined castle should be. To reach it you have to walk across a field, (no car park here), and when you reach this gatehouse it becomes apparent that this is going to be no pristine-lawned 'world of heritage' experience, manicured into sterility. Wigmore is exactly as it fell to pieces before the Civil War, with the upper floors allowed to collapse to first floor level. The arch of the gatehouse is still in position below the guardroom, albeit with rubble filling half its depth. The whole thing is a perfect example of 'pleasing decay', but decay that has been arrested with the absolute minimum of tidying-up. The walls are still capped by the grass and wild plants that have protected them for four centuries. Come up here early on a bright autumn morning, with the mist clearing away through damp trees and ferns.

Baconsthorpe Castle, Norfolk The castle is a defended manor house completed by Sir Henry Heydon in 1486, with the single most impressive remains being those of the outer gatehouse, which continued as Baconsthorpe Hall long after the rest was dismantled in the 17th century. Originally there were two pepper-pot towers, one falling in 1920, after which the Hall was abandoned as a dwelling. It stands alone in wide Norfolk fields, and on this late summer evening it takes the last light on its flint and brick walls, with only the sound of distant combine harvesters for company.

holy orders

Abbey gatehouses have often fared better than the abbeys themselves, and of course many of these vast monastic institutions would still be intact if it hadn't been for Henry VIII's Draconian religious policies. The gatehouses could fulfil a defensive function (there were plenty of malcontents looking for trouble) but usually they acted as a security checkpoint that doubled up as a metaphor for power and glory. A porter's lodge would be positioned to one side, and the upper storey would often house a small chapel.

Great Gate, Bury St. Edmunds, Suffolk

> **Norman Gate, Bury St. Edmunds, Suffolk** This is the Norman Gate built by Abbot Anselm in the 12th century. What a dramatic full stop to the end of Churchgate Street, a street that's filled with good buildings anyway. It served as a campanile to St.James' church, and up until the 19th century, it still had its original battlements.

>> **Great Gate, Bury St. Edmunds, Suffolk** This was once home to one of the greatest abbeys in Europe. A place of mummified corpses and pilgrimages, it fell into ruin after riots in 1327. But this Great Gate, possibly built by the townspeople with plundered stone from the abbey, is still very much with us. Sitting at the bottom of Angel Hill, this is triumphant 14th–century medievalism standing foursquare and defiant, combining the decoratively ecclesiastical with practical functionality.

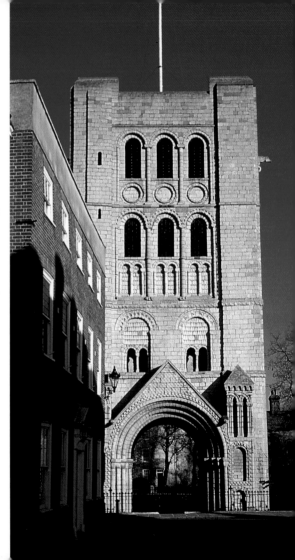

∧   **Cleeve Abbey, Somerset** The monastic remains here in Washford survived after the Dissolution thanks to their use as farm buildings by the Luttrell family from nearby Dunster, who maintained them instead of allowing them to be used as a convenient source of stone. The gatehouse is 13th century, but the last abbot, William Dovell, made considerable alterations to it in the 16th century. His motto is over the entrance: *Porta patens esto / Nulli claudaris honesto* or 'Be an open door / May you shut out no honest man'.

>   **Ramsey Abbey, Cambridgeshire** Ramsey, like Ely, was an island in the brooding fen before the great draining took place, and the abbey would have been like a lighthouse to wayfarers out in the oozing landscape. But even this remote spot couldn't avoid the relentless Dissolution, and now the principal remains from this period are the Lady Chapel and this c.1500 gatehouse; and even a large chunk of this has ended up as a gatehouse at Hinchingbrooke, ten miles away at Huntingdon. Closely shaded by yews on this quiet and hot afternoon, it felt as if the spirit had been stifled out of it, the ghosts of almoners, pardoners, prelates and lepers having long ago fled into the reeds.

initial thoughts As the threat of attack lessened, and castles evolved into country houses, gatehouses became more welcoming. Originally constructed as later additions to a principal property, (and having no stylistic links to it), by the beginning of the 17th century the first entrances were being built with variations of the design features of the houses they announced.

Stanway House, Gloucestershire A foggy January day in the Cotswolds, and emerging out of the gloom is this prodigious gatehouse to Stanway House, with its hat-like gables, scallop shells, roses, ovals and pediments. Built around 1630, it marks an era when the gatehouse was no longer the 'must have' accessory for country house owners, and when the first threatening clouds of the Civil War were gathering that would bring lodge-building virtually to a halt.

I found two other treasures in the fog: a thatched cricket pavilion on staddle stones, with a J.M.Barrie connection; and at the top of the hill, a superb and atmospheric war memorial with a St. George and the Dragon by Alexander Fisher and lettering by Eric Gill, the engraver and sculptor given to not wearing any trousers.

Stokesay Castle, Shropshire Stokesay is a perfect example of a fortified manor house, and remarkable for surviving virtually intact since the late 13th century. The main entrance is through this storybook-illustration gatehouse. Very Welsh Marches in style, the central passageway is surrounded by elaborate and decorative half-timbering and dates from around 1600. The gate itself is a robust nail-studded affair and inset with a small wicket gate. Carved figures in silvered oak stare out at the corners and from on top of the gateposts.

Chipping Campden, Gloucestershire In 1613 Sir Baptist Hickes built his showpiece house on the fringe of this north Cotswold town. Within 32 years it had been razed to the ground by retreating royalists anxious to prevent it falling into the hands of parliamentary troops. All that remains, apart from a section of fire-reddened rubble and two garden pavilions, are these Jacobean entrance lodges next to the church that contains Sir Baptist's black marble tomb chest. The ogee-shaped roofs crown what is possibly the earliest pair of entrance lodges as we now know them.

personal columns
Gatehouse-building continued after the Commonwealth period, but the late 17th century saw a fashion for the gate pier taking precedence, sometimes as the only feature at an entrance. Gate piers, of course, appear in every period, with or without attendant living quarters. Here is a selection I found when scouring the countryside for lodges.

Drayton Gate, Clumber Park, Nottinghamshire
A pedimented and rusticated pier of c.1760 by Stephen Wright, a protégé of William Kent, whose influence is so evident.

∧ **Honington, Warwickshire** Turn off the A3400 north of Shipston-on-Stour and the first clue to Honington's treasures are two pillars each side of the lane, topped with the late 17th–century fruit-of-choice, the pineapple.

> Passing over the classical bridge into the village, the open space is dominated by the gate piers to the Hall, which are a fabulous example of the Dutch style. If you like the swags and cherubs' heads, wait until you see inside the church.

∧ **Normanton Gate, Clumber Park, Nottinghamshire** This c.1700 gate pier didn't start life at Clumber. It was brought here from Shireoaks Hall in the same county, leaving only a wooden gate into a field to mark its passing.

> **Stockerston, Leicestershire** The Hall here is late 18th century, but a previous building was once served by a driveway coming down from the Medbourne road. Virtually the only reminders were a pair of c.1700 gate piers, and, like an old friend standing in the hedge, this survivor was always looked out for on the descent to the village. Suddenly, without warning, it too disappeared. I hope it's not far away.

classical prologues
Pairs of perfectly proportioned boxes are perhaps the most ubiquitous lodges of all. The names of Adam, Kent, Paine and Carr are inextricably associated with the great houses of the period, whose plans stylistically linked them to their ancillary buildings. Although the golden age for lodges was between 1740 and 1800, the classical style influenced lodge-building far into the 19th century.

Carburton Gate, Clumber Park, Nottinghamshire
The Carburton Gate hides out on the western edge of the estate. They are a delight – little pedimented Palladian lodges on a quiet road to Carburton village where it emerges from the parkland woods. Designed by Stephen Wright in the mid 18th century, they were perhaps a little 'while-you're here' job whilst he was engaged on the main house.

< **Worcester Lodge, Badminton House, Gloucestershire** It doesn't get much grander than this, a final *tour de force* from William Kent, finished after his death by Stephen Wright in 1750. It took an understanding patron, in this case the third Duke of Beaufort, to allow his architect to design something more eye-catching than his house. Suddenly and unexpectedly it appears on a bend of the A433 south west of Tetbury. Above the archway, round-headed windows on both sides light a spectacular Palladian dining room.

v **Weston Park, Staffordshire** The park lies to the south of the A5 that bisects the village of Weston Lizard, now mercifully quieter since motorways have taken away much of the traffic. The road passes two identical lodges, one to the east and this companion to the west. For gate lodges the accommodation is particularly generous, and they retain all the classical hallmarks of recessed arches and pediments. James Paine was busy working for the owner, Sir Henry Bridgeman, in the 1760s, and these lodges are assumed to have been part of his contract.

Tern Lodge, Attingham Park, Shropshire The Shrewsbury approach to Attingham Hall has John Nash's version of a triumphal arch on the A5 in the village of Atcham, but more rewarding is the smaller Tern Lodge further eastwards on the same road. A very crisp octagon projects rectangles from alternate faces, one of which, the porch, now opens straight out onto the carriageway. It was commissioned in 1802 by the second Lord Berwick from John Adey Repton.

Rokeby Park, Durham The main A66
screams by Rokeby (pronounced *Rookby*)
with everyone hell-bent on either Penrith
or Scotch Corner. The motorist in a hurry
probably won't register the pedimented gate
piers and church; the delights of Rokeby need
a little time to reveal themselves. Down a lane
at the side of the gorgeous apricot-coloured
mansion is this little classical box – not a
grand entrance, but a perfect complement
to a house in the purest of Palladian taste.
Rokeby gives its name to Velásquez's *Rokeby
Venus* that once graced the walls here and
is now in the National Gallery in London.

∧ **Easton Neston, Northamptonshire** This late 17th–century house owes much of its exterior appearance to that enigmatic architect, Nicholas Hawksmoor, but these sadly neglected lodges opening onto a road in Towcester are by John Raffield. They were built around 1822, and now suffer the indignity of painted-on windows instead of the real thing.

< The strange elliptical decoration has caused some puzzlement, but it is a very Adam-style ornament. Raffield worked with the architect in his London office in the 1770s, and the entrance upon the hill outside Towcester is influenced by Adam's screen at Syon House.

South Lodges, Holkham Hall, Norfolk This pair of 19th–century lodges sit on the South Drive to the Hall, in line with the Triumphal Arch and the limestone obelisk erected, it is thought, to mark the start of the building works. They were designed by Teulon in 1847, and still house gate keepers who unlock the gates in answer to a 'phone call from the Hall over two miles away. The signpost opposite the lodges is there purely to direct departing guests.

arch rivals The arch as an announcement finds its precedent in Roman triumphalism and in echoes of castle and abbey gatehouses. Many survive without attendant lodges, often mounted with rampant animalia, but here we will stick to those that have living quarters contained within them, or at least nearby.

Easton Neston, Northamptonshire The screen on the hill. South of Towcester is this archway flanked by two rows of Corinthian columns that stretch out to two porter's lodges. Well known to punters as the entrance to Towcester Racecourse off the A5, it is by William Croggan and was built in Coade stone in 1822, a remarkably convincing artificial stone produced by Coade and Sealey of London. One of the best known examples of the material is the lion on the south side of Westminster Bridge.

Brocklesby Park, Lincolnshire This is remote Lincolnshire, although not that far from Grimsby and the oil refineries on the Humber. Brocklesby has everything wealthy patronage could possibly bestow: fertile farmland, an estate village and cottages, a family mausoleum, a hunt and a railway station. Out on the fringes are lodges, including this barge-boarded example on the road to Kirmington. The Memorial Arch is inscribed: 'To Charles Anderson Worsley 2nd Earl of Yarborough by his Tenants and Friends 1864.'

Deene Park, Northamptonshire Deene was the country residence of Lord Cardigan, the 'Homicidal Earl' who led the Charge of the Light Brigade. Doubtless he rode Ronald (the same horse that took him down a Crimean valley on that fateful October day in 1854) through this arch after hunting with the Pytchley, perhaps exchanging a few brief words with the porter. Ronald's head now stares out with a surprised look from a wall in the house. The gateway is by John Crake, emblazoned with the Brudenell arms and erected in 1841 on what is now the A43 Stamford to Kettering road.

Triumphal Arch, Holkham Hall, Norfolk Holkham is an austere Palladian mansion built in local gault brick and set in a vast park, so close to the gunmetal blue line of the North Sea but turning its back on it. The plans for this Triumphal Arch were drawn up in 1739 for Thomas Coke by William Kent, and finally realised by Matthew Brettingham in 1752. It uses the same yellow brick as the Hall, but here it is embellished to great effect with rustication made from whole flints – a vernacular Norfolk building material if ever there was one.

Harlaxton Manor, Lincolnshire Pevsner said that the towering mass of Harlaxton '... must be seen to be believed.' A monster of a house in a startling mix of the Elizabethan and the Baroque, a 32-year-old Anthony Salvin designed it in the 1830s for the mysterious Gregory Gregory. It even had its own railway for delivering coal into the back quarters. Halfway down an undulating drive that passes the kitchen gardens is this baronial Tudor gatehouse, possibly also by Salvin. Peter O'Toole galloped his horse maniacally through it in Peter Medak's epic film, *The Ruling Class*.

Audley End, Essex All eyes settle from afar on the Earl of Suffolk's mansion, so the gate lodges can be easily overlooked. This is the Lion Gate, with a patently glum-looking lion staring west, his tail pointing accusingly back at Saffron Walden. He is made from Coade stone, an 18th–century imitation stone for which the specifications have been lost. The gate was erected in 1786 in anticipation of a visit from George III. He didn't turn up, and so never passed through the new arch or slept in the bedroom prepared for him and Queen Charlotte in the house. The 1846 red brick porter's lodge was designed by the Gothic Revivalist architect, Thomas Rickman.

lost hearts

lost hearts All too often entrance lodges are virtually the only surviving buildings on country estates. We lost so many houses in the first half of the 20th century it was a national disgrace. Many literally fell down from neglect after punitive death duties were enforced, others burst into flames, and many were thought not worth saving after the ravages of wartime use. So now the only reminders of former glories may be a stable block or lonely lodges on drives leading nowhere.

Apleyhead Lodge, Clumber Park, Nottinghamshire

The big house has gone, its atmosphere clinging on like a lost ghost amongst the trees and water of extensive parkland. All that physically remains is a slightly eerie chapel, a heron-haunted bridge and a number of gateways. The largest and most impressive is the Apleyhead Lodge, standing on the A614 close to its junction with the A1. Stephen Wright designed this spectacular sweep of arch and lodges for the second Duke of Newcastle in 1778. It must have been a curious sensation to live inside lodges built on such a dramatic curve, watching from the windows for impending departures to emerge from out of the three-mile avenue of limes.

Blatherwyke, Northamptonshire This 1876 lodge survived when the Hall was sadly demolished in 1948, along with so many after the deprivations caused by their requisitioning in wartime. In her *Shell Guide*, Juliet Smith gets it exactly right when imagining the coaches of the Staffords and O'Brians rumbling homewards down a drive that '...would provide an ideal setting for the opening of an M.R. James ghost story.' Perhaps accompanied by the melancholy sound of the hurdy-gurdy from his chilling tale, *Lost Hearts*.

∧ **Tittenley Lodges, Shavington Hall, Shropshire** Remote, lonely lanes
surround a sprawling park that has long lost its Hall. I didn't see another soul for
an hour until caught poking my nose over a wall on another side of the estate. It
took some time to find these 1885 neo-Georgian lodges in pale orange brick and
I couldn't help thinking they looked like a pair of police houses, probably because
they were designed by Norman Shaw, who occasionally did that kind of thing.

> **Stoke Edith, Herefordshire** Stoke Edith Park was gutted by fire in 1927, but here
on the A438 between Hereford and Ledbury is a surviving lodge. The dome could
be a tricky thing even in 1792, but this is a very successful example by William
Wilkins, who designed the National Gallery. A central chimney stack becomes a
copper-domed roof, which becomes an octagon that sprouts projections that
effectively give it sixteen sides. Some Tuscan columns are then inset for good
measure. In the 1950s it apparently fooled passers-by with a trompe d'oeil sash
window, complete with painted lace curtains and geraniums on a sill.

great pretenders
Lodges were unmissable opportunities to build theatrical announcements to houses, and could easily mutate into storybook castles and mock-Gothic chapels. And then there was the fashion for mixing and matching architectural styles from previous ages, resulting in medieval towers built in the 18th century and Jacobean entrances in the 19th century.

Rushton Hall, Northamptonshire The Hall is mostly associated with Sir Thomas Tresham, a Catholic recusant who built coded buildings to express his faith. (On the same estate is his wonderful Triangular Lodge). These gate lodges to the east of the house, dating from around 1820, symbolise something else: a desire to make simple buildings appear to be what they're not – in this case Gothic chapels.

Burghley House, Stamford, Lincolnshire Ministers and confidants of Elizabeth I tended to go in for prodigious house building, and William Cecil, later Lord Burghley, was no exception. His monumental house, which was in construction throughout the late 16th century, is of awe-inspiring proportions, and the west gates are a perfect complement, except they were built in 1801, designed by W.D.Legg. Known locally as the Bottle Lodges, this neo-Jacobean entrance opens onto the old Great North Road, just before what Sir Walter Scott said was the finest view between London and Edinburgh. It still is, as the road starts its descent into stone-built Stamford.

< Gayhurst, Buckinghamshire This estate has much to be proud of: an Elizabethan mansion, a classic George II church with an imposing monument, and a famous walnut tree. This little lodge can easily be missed, hiding behind trees and shrubs on the busy B526 near Newport Pagnell. It started out as an 18th–century lodge, converting to mock-Elizabethan with two turrets in 1882. I remember drinking here when it took on another life as a pub called the Sir Francis Drake, named after the bowls-playing mariner who was given an earlier house here after a successful world tour.

<< Edgehill Tower, Warwickshire This 1747 gingerbread conceit was built as a scene-setter at the top of a precipitous drive that provided a hair-raising coach ride down to Radway Grange. I like to think that one of the first to enjoy it was Henry Fielding, who came here to read the manuscript of his rollicking novel, *Tom Jones*. The embattled tower was designed by antiquarian, Sanderson Miller, sited where the King's standard was raised prior to the Civil War battle of 23 October, 1642.

rustic charms The late 18th and early
19th centuries saw a fashion for picturesque lodges,
helping along the craze for all things rustic. Not the
reality of tumbled-down, rat-infested workers' hovels
of course, although designer ruins with deliberately
trained ivy were OK. No, this was one of those
occasions when the lodge looked exactly what it
always was – a cottage.

Roxton Hall, Bedfordshire Many *cottage ornée*-
style lodges would not look out of place in an edition
of Grimms' Fairy Tales, and here in a Bedfordshire
park is a perfect example. With a tall hat of thatch
on wooden supports that still look like tree trunks,
this was perhaps home to Rumpelstiltskin.

∧ **Stapleford Park, Leicestershire** A thatched lodge on the west side of the park, next to spectacular horseless stables. Barge-boarding on the eaves was often a feature of the cottage style, and this elaborately carved example contrasts sharply with the much simpler rough stone used for the walls and the dressed stone of the window frames.

< **Snarehill Hall, Norfolk** You've really got to be looking out for this one, as concentration ought to be on the A1066 to either Thetford or Diss. I imagine it was once thatched, but the pantiled roof, with its flint-faced chimney stack, and the yellow stucco walls stand well against the pines. But just look at that dormer window; it's as though the glaziers had held a competition on a Friday afternoon to see how many individual panes of glass could be fitted into a single frame.

Ashton Wold, Northamptonshire
To the architecturally minded this is
the entrance lodge to Lord Rothschild's
house, the centrepiece of his brand new
estate and village, built in 1900. Every
cottage had a bathroom and electricity
supplied from wires laid underground.
But to everyone here, it's Murder
Cottage. George and Lillian Peach lived
here in 1952, 480 yards from the village,
until in the early hours of 25th October
they were bludgeoned to death with a
coal hammer. No one has ever been
apprehended, and it still remains one
of the great unsolved murder mysteries,
even though Scotland Yard travelled up
the same day.

Lodge Cottage, Pertenhall, Bedfordshire A perfect example of the genre, and, unusually, a lodge built at the entrance to a country rectory. Pertenhall is where Bedfordshire starts to drift into East Anglia proper, where the vernacular architecture in the landscape often features colour-washed cottages. Lodges rarely reflect their natural surroundings, usually being the realisation of a patron's dream and an architect's plan, but here the lodge is very comfortably at home amongst the lupins and chestnuts.

gothic revivalists

The Victorian age ushered in a wealth of mock-medieval style. So enamoured were its chief exponents, they started to live in what they considered to be a glorious past. Augustus Welby Pugin took his Gothic fads to extreme heights, eating his meals from Gothic plates, dressing his women up in Gothic frocks (nothing wrong with that), and signing up to Roman Catholicism because that's how it was in the 15th century. Everything contrived to take on the mantle of medievalism: railway stations, memorials, Parliament, schools, offices, houses, and of course, their lodges.

Milton Hall, Peterborough The remarkable thing about this Gothic lodge is that it's an appreciable distance from where it was first built. The approach from the south was originally across a three-arched bridge that still spans the River Nene, and after crossing the main Leicester to Peterborough road, this lodge was passed on the way to the Hall. When the A47 was considerably widened and made into a dual carriageway, it was moved wholesale up out of harm's way.

Thunderdell Lodge, Ashridge, Hertfordshire Ashridge is private, actually a management college (watch out for Competitive Men sweating through the undergrowth), but the National Trust owns much of the surrounding parkland. The house itself is a Gothic colossus, but out on the south western approaches is this lodge, altogether more subdued and appealing. The flint chequerwork is very much at home with the beeches, a feature often found on churches in chalk country.

Wadenhoe, Northamptonshire At first glance, this little building has all the hallmarks of a toll house, but the lane to the right only leads down to the village inn, straight on descends to a thundering mill race, and to the left is the drive for Wadenhoe House, a house with 17th–century beginnings but now really 1858 Victorian. And the polygonal window bay of this lodge is perfectly placed to keep an eye on it all.

<< **Leigh, Kent** Hall Place in Leigh
<<< (pronounced *Lie*) is a Victorian restoration of an Elizabethan red-brick original which was badly damaged by fire. To restore it took the wealth of an industrialist, Samuel Morley, and his programme of rebuilding that included re-shaping the village and building these Gothic lodges with diapered brickwork and stone quoins at the angles. They can be found on the B2027 just west of Tonbridge.

< **Childwickbury, Hertfordshire** This is one of those lodges that brings all those who love these things to a screeching halt. I found it by accident, being hopelessly lost in Hertfordshire, although it's obviously well known to everybody who regularly travels on the A1081 between St. Albans and Harpenden. It once welcomed a masterful and reclusive film director to his home, and doubtless he appreciated this juggling display of red brick and terracotta.

Back Lodge, Attingham Park, Shropshire For all the impressive grandeur of prodigious country houses, it is often the smaller detail that catches and pleases the eye. From the main driveway I spotted this little Gothic lodge away amongst the trees across the park. Closer inspection revealed the handful of features that have added so much to a simple cottage: battlements, quatrefoiled openings and pointed arches did the trick, with a well thought-out paint scheme bringing them all together.

North Lodge, Eaton Hall, Cheshire

Eaton Park is an extensive estate to the south of Chester, home to the Duke of Westminster, whose Grosvenor family antecedents stretch back to the Normans. Over this time a succession of houses reflecting a variety of tastes have appeared in the landscape, but it's the many lodges that continually amaze. When Alfred Waterhouse was commissioned by Hugh Lupus Grosvenor, the 1st Duke, to build a new house in 1870, he simply opted for recycling his designs for Manchester Town Hall. The 'Big Ben' clock tower still survives, the house having gone the same way as its equally unloved successor. But Waterhouse redeemed himself with the 1881 North Lodge, a four-storey round tower snuggled up to a stair turret that still causes distress to those wishing to move furniture about. On the upper storey gable is a sunflower, the motif of the Aesthetic Movement that was to influence so much of what was going on elsewhere on the estate.

crafty exits All those church windows and dreaming spirelets started to wear a bit thin towards the end of the 19th century, and a handful of architects began to look at simpler, less cluttered forms of expression. Norman Shaw built Bedford Park in Chiswick to look like a Queen Anne market town, and later the talents of architects like Edwin Lutyens and Charles Voysey brought natural materials back in vernacular-influenced designs. They weren't copies of old buildings, just imbued with their spirit and character, and they became as much a part of the new Arts and Crafts movement as fabrics and book illustration. Brick, plaster, half-timbering and tile-hanging combined in a farmhouse style that often suited the lodges more than the houses.

Aldford Gate Lodge, Eaton Hall, Cheshire Most gate lodges are easily seen from public highways, but Eaton is very private and many are sadly out of bounds. One that isn't is the gate lodge in one of the three estate villages, Aldford. John Douglas was a local architect who was bringing the new fashion for romantic Arts and Crafts designs to his Cheshire commissions. When you see his imaginative work on the Eaton Lodges you can't help wondering what his ideas for an Eaton Hall would have looked like. On this late spring day the maintenance teams were out, putting the final touches to the Westminster decoration on the lodge gable. By the painter's left hand can be seen the Arts and Crafts sunflower motif.

Eccleston Hill Lodge, Eaton Hall, Cheshire Of all his work for the Duke, which was considerable, John Douglas' 1881–82 Eccleston Hill Lodge is the one to take your breath away. Brick and tile-hung turrets spring up from duotone sandstone studded with Grosvenor heraldry, everything contrasting with the Cheshire magpie half-timbering. Hidden now, isolated out in the park on the old approach from Chester, it is so evocative of another age I have to quote from Tim Mowl and Brian Earnshaw's invaluable *Trumpet at a Distant Gate*: '(it appears) to link forest with green forest like a sudden enchantment from the *Morte d'Arthur* or the *Faerie Queene*.'

Victoria Park, Leicester The War Memorial in Leicester is a massive flat-domed arch by Sir Edwin Lutyens, erected in the park in 1923. Ten years later he returned with two park lodges joined by a wrought-iron gate supporting the distinctive city badge. Very Lutyens, very Leicester how it used to be. Each lodge is divided into four pavilions, each with a flat pyramidical roof and characteristic over-sized chimney stacks.

Park Hatch, Hascombe, Surrey The 1889 South Sussex Lodge at Park Hatch was Lutyens' first crack at lodge design. Still under the influence of his employer, Ernest George, he picked up the idea of purely decorative half-timbering from George & Peto's Onslow Almshouses in Guildford. But, in what is actually a pair of lodges, Lutyens' architectural ideas are starting to emerge, picked up from his study (with Gertrude Jekyll) of West Surrey vernacular buildings. With wooden Doric pillars on the loggias and small-scale cottage windows, they were built using prize money won with Sussex cattle.

Norney Grange, Shackleford, Surrey Amongst Charles Annesley Voysey's fervently held views was the belief that houses should embody 'Quietness in a storm, Harmony with surroundings.' His designs for the Reverend Leighton Grane at Norney Grange, in roughcast and yellow limestone, were superbly adapted for this 1897 lodge, one of two hiding amongst the rhododendrons. This was the last lodge I photographed for this book and, as I drove off to join the noisesome A3, a glance in the mirror revealed nothing but dark trees surrounding the front gable with its oriel bay window. Walter de la Mare's *The Listeners* came to mind, 'And how the silence surged softly backward...'

acknowledgements Many kind people have helped me with this book. I would particularly like to thank all those lodge dwellers who made me welcome or put up with me lurking about outside their homes. At Everyman: David Campbell, Sandra Pisano and Clémence Jacquinet. At Anikst Design: James Warner and Misha Anikst. At English Heritage: Val Horsler and Simon Bergin. Dr.Tim Mowl at Bristol University. The agents at the Eaton Estate Office and Peter Cave at Peter Cave Associates. Mary James for a quick bit of Latin. The Curator's Office at Burghley House. Stephen Coleman at Bedfordshire County Council. James Bowdidge, Rupert Farnsworth and Elizabeth Raven-Hill.

bibliography *Trumpet at a Distant Gate*, Tim Mowl and Brian Earnshaw, Waterstone 1985. *The Buildings of England Series*, Penguin Books. *The Shell County Guides*, Faber & Faber.

< **Shavington Hall, Shropshire** Cheshire vernacular in a solitary lodge for a long lost Hall.

Overleaf:
Pipewell Hall, Northamptonshire A tiny village that hides away from the sprawling mass of Corby, not three miles away. Long may the evening fire be lit here in solitude.